VIA Folios 158

D1636752

Also by Julia Lisella

Always

Terrain

Love Song, Hiroshima

Our Lively Kingdom

TABLE OF CONTENTS

I

II

III

IV

I

Our Lively Kingdom

Our lively kingdom's now broken
into village plots that others love to visit.

The Happiness plot rendered through
refuse of the old argument
and memory of two bodies pressed by sheer heat.

Perennials and herbs grace the kitchen window
of its sweet cottage
but really almost anything can grow here—even last year's annuals
come shunting through with a tiny roar.

Long Distance

I'm listening to him
listen to me over the cell phone line

a low *shwoosh* of small stories
meant to close a gap in time we'll have

when I return. My voice a slow trickle
like rivulets of river water over stones.

I watch a bird darting in the underbrush
as I tell him a story of our daughter's phone call to me.

He responds by telling me he is staring
out the back window of our kitchen

at our dog on our porch who is staring at a bird
in our backyard. He heads outside to put the phone

to the dog's ear to see if he will recognize my voice.
He says the sound of me

does not recall me for the dog. I laugh.
He says *mmmm* which is different than *hmmm*.

Marriage Bed

The marriage bed is a village of strange love
where knowledge grows less sharp, less exact.

Ghost or spirit-guided, the bodies follow
as friends might follow each other's shadows in the too-dark theater.

One feels the other there, one knows the other's patter of footfall
on the dirty carpet. Likewise, the bodies

torque and form their nighttime language, each limb a small animal
seeking comfort, sustenance.

Somewhat deep in the dream of each of our nights
there's a small hurt that renders meaning.

Caress lingers on the sheets, a light dusting,
and the day begins again, un-remembering and un-making

that which must be felt again each night, the question repeating
and the question being answered.

Poems for My Birthday

I.

On November 6, 1962, I was exactly one, held in the arms
of a mother of four. I was the fourth, the chubbiest, the stillest,
easy to manage. She placed me inside the carriage. Fixed the blanket
with her eyes on something else. She hurried inside to finish her work
and did not watch the slow trio, my grandfather pushing the carriage,
flanked by the curious black-haired 3-year-old girl,
grey-eyed, like the doe, unflinching. That day, as my *nonno* strolled us
up and down 246th Street in Bellerose, Queens, Sylvia Plath wrote
     three poems
in her cold London flat. It *was* cold. We can know this now.
My sister hummed. My grandfather squinted at the unusual
November sun, each of us bundled in '60s flannel.
My mother wanting to nap but no, scrubbing a pot, delivering a cup
     of tea
to my cranky grandmother, figuring out dinner. She stands still for
     a minute,
rubs her palms against the sides of her apron. She isn't thinking
much. But she can feel the afternoon waning.
My grandfather has returned with the two of us and there are
so many next things to do.

II.

When my mother was 57 I was 15. Fives plagued us that year,
five decades, five kinds of ways of dying. We died a little from
each other. Her marriage and everything that could slip
did, tangling on the floor at our feet. This is my birthday today.
Today *I* am 57. My mother does not call to wish me a happy birthday.
She has forgotten. When I call will she tell me the story?
how easily I came, an afterthought, a bright accidental penny,
something good that grew around her like protective uncomplicated
     vines?

She noticed blossoms here and there but liked the vine as well
in winter, in the depths of stillness, the child, to the woman,
to the bowing branch. The sound of our wheels
on the crackling ice of 83rd Avenue returning
—doctor, dentist, department store—
we'd burrow into books and television, and cooking.

I'd shadow her.

III.

Gulliver, too?
Did Plath write this one last in the day, about the monster on his back?
Was she thinking of tyranny, of giant hands holding her
or of the sound of the name so close to gullible, gully, Gullah, gulag?
At the same time I'd reached baby hands to the sky to be lifted out
    of the carriage
she'd been raising hers, manicured and perfect, perhaps to the wrong god.
Gulliver did not understand what way his present body
could be scorched and tortured by the less powerful,
and yet there he was, abandoned to a parallel world of moon and stars,
of desires that were no longer his exactly.
When the phone rings I think I won't answer it, but then I do. It is
my mother, in fact, and indeed she's called to say
her leg hurts and she is worried about my daughter.
The baby in the carriage learned well; I close the door again
now that she is too old to receive me.

Octave

The car's a flimsy capsule
I realize as   I   try   to
drive   and   to   sing

Where should I start?

My son the singer
                              anywhere
Growing up

              8

was my favorite number

I try to reach it first

That's not even a third
          maybe 2 ½   laughing

I'm still driving us forward

but my voice pausing
              yielding
backward—the car seemingly
moving without me

                                                                    e
                                                      dooooooo

I start again—singing
makes me drive more slowly—

                                                            -

Once, twice, and again

                                          -

I hit

the octave—doe

I drag the high "doe" out

to be sure I've hit it

to convince myself

In time, the boy beside me

amused
amazed that what floats
easily between his lips
is hard work for this woman
who bore him

My hands grip the wheel—what is
the direction of the octave—

a low and a high but the same—?
a mystery to me
as all music is

Is there an octave in the poem
I break–remake–consume
without effort?

The car our shared oxygen—
        our guide
now dangerous
        it needs guiding

The road
on its own cannot be laid out in octaves

And love

certainly

not like an octave at all

or maybe—the low the high the same? but driving is different

and we push ahead—

pace & mastery at odds
my hands grip the wheel

I try again to hit the note but can't complete it

I navigate through a bad pass
from 93 to 95—show my son
the way
the breakdown lane

becomes a fine place to travel
with permission

Some Loved Object

Now here, now there, the roving Fancy *flies,*
Till some lov'd object strikes her wand'ring eyes...

Phillis Wheatley, "On Imagination"

She was the master
weaver
could thread hair, silk, leather
could speak even when
not spoken to
could conjure quietly
she had a mistress

but she was master
of the penned things that rose
above her desk—their lamplight song
the messengers—
reported her goings on silently

first, they bought her   home,   a little girl
to name and feed, to teach the Bible to
she so
quiet in her bonnet

and then they led her nightly to
her song she threatening to break
books' bindings
pages bound but open

just like her to

She understood that it was *Winter* that kept her mostly
while *Fancy* kicked up the loose dirt around the cobblestones
of 18th century Boston
> where She was free to roam and write. I had never been to
> Boston

when I read the skinny paperback, its yellowed pages
I was fevered, maybe 9 years old

both my grandparents died
in the room where I began to read
of Phillis
born poet, stolen from Senegal. Of her mother? No.
Her father: a prince, a king, a farmer?

As remote to me as Jane Eyre—only Phillis fixed
in history while the other
lived only in *Fancy*
or were they both of *Winter* made?

Phillis married and died. And in her marriage it's possible
she never wrote again, or maybe wrote the songs of the truly

loved object, but what it was, I didn't learn that day
fevered and full of love

for the Girl who'd done slavery
so spectacularly

Mercy

She draws her lines with a dull pencil
while others fold their sheets of paper
evenly in four
sharpening creases with stubby fingers

She likes the way her sections
divide unevenly
and force each drawing of the 4 seasons
into secret rooms

When the teacher shifts
between the rows
collecting the children's pages
this girl will not say *no*

but will hand it over
as if she knows already that the slight shame she feels
should not be hidden
What has she done she wonders?

Her page floats above the others
her winter drawn widely with loose strokes
her spring pinched
its lines crashing the corners to fit

Charlotte's Zinnias

Each pop of brazen orange or hot pink quivers
as Charlotte's legs cross over her hand-made fence
her basket following in the mess of multicolored swiss chard
and flowering basil. I head the tops of the green stalks
as we talk of the zinnias, amazing and flourishing.
Bees. Their deaths and births discussed.
And chard. How you can freeze it. Charlotte
knows how to enjoy a good day
as they come less often in New England Augusts when you're 83.
How can you not *love the summer?* Charlotte says
recommending I take one more short-cut
neon bath of zinnia into my dirty fist. And also she's reading a book
about Chekov and how he became Chekov
which is a novel she says, a story about what he might have been
before *The Cherry Orchard*, and also
he never wrote a novel though he'd intended to.
I suppose that's a fact inside the novel I must read.

It's good, as we pick more zinnias and chard, my grip loosening,
that Chekov might be a person who was not yet himself
ambling, showing up at a person's house to rent it for the summer
in this time or a time before, and Charlotte
an old woman in his time or mine. That's

what is left in my head when I remove the small beat up
zinnia that could not stand with the others.
And as I snip the others at tight slants for each end to absorb more water
I am smiling on an August day while the old tip of a most pink
zinnia leaps somewhat across the sink.

No Heaven

All day I hear my own words
like the fancy words of a precocious kid
that kind of annoying. *No heaven.* This is it. We have to
get it right.

And then at night I think *yeah right, we have to*
but the day's gone badly. I yelled at my dear old mom,
94 and all her wits, as she said she's all there but wishes
she wasn't. And I kept saying *no heaven*
and there she was with her tiny face searching

mine the way she used to to see if I'd been to church
or just said so. As though she knew that earlier that day
in the parking lot of the Barnes & Nobles
the wind flapping in our faces, our son distracted and
walking ahead of us through traffic

my husband and I had looked at each other after
smashing car doors behind us and said it together
there is no heaven psyche
this is it baby this is it.

Poem for Our 31 Years Together

Ever since I learned
that Julia Child's favorite snack after a long day at the set
was a martini and McDonald's French fries, shared with her beloved Paul
    while the fries were still hot she'd recommended
        don't fold the paper bag over the little cardboard box
with the idea to keep them crispy, each fry wrapped in its salt and
    meat grease,
the stored heat there to match the cold freeze of the vodka,
I knew our path was set. I am not sure how many olives she'd prescribed,
though for us they are like a briny vegetable pairing to the full meal
cornered by tongue and glass,
a couple, like us.

Bird Walk

On the wire woven through the trees
the bird—gray, larger than a swallow—
lands, seems frantic

to hear a call returning her high caw.

I stop beneath the tree
half thinking
we are waiting together

but my dog grows impatient
tugs for the next sniff near the end of the block
he, too, feeding on breath
and instinct and I let him
tug me along.

But I keep listening behind me
for the distance between
the end of the bird's one high shriek and then another
turn to see the slight cock of her head
as she waits for sound to be met by sound
a companion
who does not seem to be anywhere near.

What waiting is is never clear
but I can feel it now
as something close
to this lost sound
a vibration nearly recovered and nearly returned
to the original vibration
the original shrill of need or love.

Love Visits Us

after Sylvia Plath's "Kindness"

O *Love,* you flat-footed, awkward girl,
you sit at a table too short
for your long arms, your bony elbows,

waiting for us grownups to speak to each other, but we are busy
eating, paying bills, marking our books with dog ears.
Bored or terrified you push yourself away again, fingers lifting

one by one from the table, and absently touch your face.
Outside, you keep walking, the sky a blue you swear you have
never seen before. In summer

you are surer of yourself; you briefly warm me
with a tight embrace so that I remember
how it's always been. But in winter, *Love*, you

are more silent, perhaps shy, embarrassed
to take me with you into the core of things,
into the press of familiar arms, into the breath

of the man you held out to me so many years ago
when I, too, was a summer girl.

Beginnings, in December

When I press my fingertips together and make
a tangerine-size space that the light comes through

I see God there a little bit—a glowy something

I try to press deeper in
past the flesh and bone

my breath pulls into it to hold it there
deeper   stiller
and I worry about dying then

about how my small cradle of energy   of light   of what I think is God

will bounce along quietly and suddenly
into a new space

who will remember
how I cry all through Advent

and cry for not remembering

each other light

each cradle I have shaped

                    been shaped by

II

Community Garden

The garden has a lock
and the combination is
secret.

The fence is as high
as my waist.

Someone climbed it
last night—Bud Light
royal blue cans and
one large Heineken silver
and green.

I left them snug
between the tomatoes
and the chokecherries
seeded from my neighbor's plot

for others to find, for others to report.
I'm done reporting.

I'm done respecting fences
that can be climbed over,
maybe that should be.

Saint Nothing

Between the leaves of the trees
the white lust of sunlight enters

my *now* a cord I wrap around the ones I love

to wrap the story sweet and tight of how we may have met
were made to love each other.

>   Saint of Nothing, how you bless me
>   how you intercede for me

>   intercede now as I forget how to land my feet
>   discern the weather, tell a good lie or a bad truth.

Let me venerate you today.

Let me make offerings at your dirty little table at the back of the café.

Why must I seek you out?

Turn off the lights, Saint Nothing, and hum to me
until I fall asleep. Then walk out quietly
and do not return.

I will not mourn you as I've mourned
my body's puzzle
its strange heat, prickled skin
    it is what I wore to the party
you've said. You stand quietly by.

Saint Nothing, why stay to remind me what will be. Saint of
Nothing, my cry is a full belting song now. My friends
        who will be dying before me.

The man beside me, the children
you'll make me abandon.
> What is your plan? To gain your sainthood you suffered how?
After all, losing nothing is nothing.

Anger

Anger is as sure a signal of love as smoke is of fire.
Rev. Dr. Maggie Arnold

*Cease from anger, and forsake wrath: fret not yourself
in any way to do evil.*
Psalm 37:8, *King James 2000*

When I bend down to hear the rosemary grow

half shadowed from the sun

    struggling for its green scent

I want to strike a blow to each hand carrying a torch

that lights a village somewhere—

    I want anger because I want

what I've been warned to avoid

I want to do evil

    to evil. The scent of rosemary still on my fingers
        I roll the needles through my palms

the more I need it, I feel the more that it will grow.

Hot Flash

I breathe through,
turn my head away from the clerk while speaking,
or fan myself while on the phone chatting. My nose to the dog,
my wet forehead on his paw. Or stare at the fan
spinning above my head. 5:30 a.m. I am not just my body
I insist while the passage of heat makes its way
familiar journey now from some no place before the earth was formed
to my neck and face, my outer limbs
a deep sweat—a swooning—so miraculous yet it happens
several times a day—
is my body just grieving
the loss of the blood-red moons,
the cramps, the muscles throbbing?
Some days I swear
I feel the swell at the breast
as though I'm due to feed my kid.
The body's history feels different than mine
as does the earth's, and yet in unison
we keep telling this short story without words
with spasm and fit   like lyric   like labor.

Maternal Half-Life

for Orlando and for the Others

In the illustration above, 50% of the original mother substance decays into a new daughter substance. After two half-lives, the mother substance will decay another 50%, leaving 25% mother and 75% daughter. A third half-life will leave 12.5% of the mother and 87.5% daughter. In reality, daughter substances can also decay, so the proportions of substance involved will vary.

From "What is Meant By Half-Life"

Mornings have their half-lives as surely Mourning
does. Morning light's half-life streams in as if
torn from night. First light becomes sunrise
into lives not yet ready. And already the light
divides and divides into the day while Mourning
shakes and shakes, trying to itself achieve half of half of half
which is infinite, bottomless,
like the bang, the plume of the machine gun
of the mad young man at odds with the body that made him
dividing and dividing the pure bodies of the 49 around him
into the halves of halves of halves of morning light.
And left in the doorways, the living rooms, the cramped kitchens,
are Mourning's half-lives halved and halved and without end,
like the half-life of the labor pain
that circles, returns, but does not diminish,
until the torso radiant with light amazes and releases
its others whose half-lives cleave and divide again.

Morning After: A.M. Commute Day After the Presidential Election of 2016

Wednesday morning though Route 2 was dense in traffic
cars seemed to be floating

Not drifting or purposeless, but somehow lighter, other worldly
moving with a kind of extra-real force

In the rear view I studied another driver's face
brilliant and still, not distracted or blank as they usually seemed

At the merge to I-95, those entering 2 and exiting 2 waved our hands
curved around each other, and on the next ramp, a tight exchange
    between

those getting on 95 and those getting off, we signaled with smiles
we signaled with our eyes   *okay to pass me, okay to cut me off for the
    deep merge*

We were one slow-moving machine in a strange rapture of kindness
cars being received and cars being expelled

and in each I imagined it, the wailing, echoed and multiplied, plaintive
    and clear

A Member of the Poor

In the small house in Queens where I grew up
daylight flutters behind broken blinds
and proofs of memory
scatter across the dining table
in Post-it notes in neon colors
on which my mother writes the name of a woman
who calls her now and then
to prove her fingers still can bend around a pencil
M-I-L-L-Y in a cursive learned in school
90 years ago

my mother's pennies are disappearing into her care:
the strength of another woman
who guides her to the bathroom, wipes her
places the mashed food before her of which she always says now
agh what is this? she eats to clear the plate

the economy of care slithers down her body
while fat men in the center of things have learned
to keep their pennies near, grossing under their pornographic growth
beneath their hips
a world of poor
in a country vat of aging bodies unaccounted for

a care box arrives to my mother's house from "city meals"
canned cut vegetables and packages of albacore and salmon
and powdered milk in a small jug as though she might be
a survivalist storing up

but this is a pleasant house
with wall-to-wall carpeting and running water and daughters
calling oil men, plumbers, boys from down the block
to shovel and to fix

a system of care confuses the otherwise thinning bank account
we stare at as the checks are written to hold her body upright
to keep her body safe
nightly she watches CNN
she and her caregiver nearly spitting at the scene
where the yellow man (as her caregiver calls him) without mercy
visits again his beloved sea lake which is neither sea nor lake
a man who confesses he does not sleep and so it's clear
he does not dream—he is new here
in the country of broken bank accounts
and aging women who have saved for their lifetime
what he will spend today.

A Lesson from My Father About Manure

He said it had a sweet smell back on the farm
different from what was left in the streets of the City
when he was a boy between fruit carts and hawkers
a stuck-in-your-throat sweetness
behind the stable, out in the field, past the haystacks
on the way to milk the cows at daybreak
it was part of the grass there, just the end of what
had been a sweet beginning, green grass wet in the morning
soak-your-boots wet. The manure did not
have a bad smell he insisted
context was everything, horse shit
or cow shit on the farm was the kind of sweet
that could make you remember
could be the evidence you needed that air
could hold things, hold knowledge, hold the fortune
of a good life lived.
      Really, shit did not have a bad smell
unless it was someplace it didn't belong
on the street, dragged into your house
or stuck in the lie of someone's terrible excuse.
In those cases manure was not the perfume of farm animals
waking to sunbreak. It was a warning
you'd woken in the wrong place, the wrong life.

a brief history

we were little and we were dark
and there were so many of us
speaking our guttural dialects and unable
to speak to each other
we descended like goblins
eyes tearing from the smoke and the smells
of the ships that brought us here

we were greeted by spit and
swift tongues & in them we were
wop and guinea and grease ball
we were given a lynching and then we were given
a holiday
we were given a key to a Renaissance Italy
so we were music we were makers we were
lovers we were famous

we were Giovanna to Jenny, Pietro to Pete, Francesco to Frankie
we were Philomena to Phil, Giulio to Jules
we were quiet when the man with the ships
became a story in a history book
he had rhymes we had parades
we had a holiday from the grime and the news stories
of we the radicals we the troublemakers
we were little and we were dark

Thoughts About Hunger on a Morning Walk

All life is like that
a pursuit to satiate hunger

hunger for love hunger for food hunger for
. . .   and in pursuing it
not beauty but violence
which eats that hunger

persistent

as the ants in the cleave of sink

the wasps boring out of the hole in the ground

the dog whining for the company
of some mammal nearby

the squirrel carrying half a bagel
across the lawn and in a flash

dropping it
in pursuit of another catch

more life in which to pursue
hunger

the lady in nightshorts
watering the lamppost and the curved brick edging

while the grass beneath her slippers
yearns

this is the way we trick ourselves
decorating the hunger with potted plants and plastic figurines

my text to my son 200 miles away
have a good day I love you

which is not a real greeting but the hunger to lift him again
in my arms as he once was

even my mother at 97 still feeding me
her hunger, her worry, her thirst

her arms nearly breakable in sleep
joints no longer connecting
elbow knees and toes

parrying, contemplating—these are just fillers
like so much refuse on the shore line of a city beach

evidence that we lived, broke open a beer
relished a drumstick or an apple—cores and bones

washing up reminding us of hunger

now at the kitchen sink the miniscule ants march
ferociously into the sprayed Raid

as if each still in life, still in pursuit
still hungry.

Faculty Development Workshop

Do you know the sound of the gun?
One person raises his hand.

Locate. Leave. Live.
There is another rule, but I forget the "L" word for it,
Lock? It will make all the difference,
but I can't remember it. There is *Barricade*.
That's put all your junk up the wall—
and it will take that much longer for the *bad guy,*
he says *bad guy,* to get in with his gun.
But that is a "B," and I don't know the "L,"
and now I'm breathing fast
during this demonstration, trying to
relocate from my memory the fourth "L" that will
make all the difference.

Do you know much about guns?
Know the kinds of sounds each kind of gun can make?
No one raises their hand in this little Northeastern college.
Do you know how to hunt? Anyone here hunt?
Do you know how to be hunted? *You should run.*

When should we run? After we have locked the door?
No, it depends.
When the sound of the gun is far away, you can run,
or you can stay. Really, you can stay.
You only need 15 minutes of safety. That's all.
In 15 minutes, he says, the cops will have arrived.
Let's watch this demonstration of a man
trying to break down the wall in a classroom
in which the door has been barricaded.
The classroom is six floors up, so there is no *Leaving*. We are working on
Live. Do you know the force of a man against a wall

barricaded with desks and empty filing cabinets and the pressure
of your feet against the chairs?
It may take 4.34 minutes, which is a good long time
to prepare to do the next thing, which is, in this case,
not to *Leave*, as this is not an option,
but to *Live*,
which is the one we are working on right now
when the gun pops into the door, between the barricade
and us. There is more to the video;
there is more to the reenactment. The barricade's fallen,
and my heart's still pounding. If only I could remember
the fourth "L," as *Locate, Leave,* and *Live*
have taken me as far as I can go now.

Before This

In one life before I was a woman
I was *a Siren*
my hair the song, the seducer
reaching to my shoulders
hanging before my eyes
covering my body and yours
nearly black and downy
in another birth
I was *Medusa*
locks of snakes
protecting the curvature of skull and bone and neck and arms
I was curse and holy thing—
        you'd come before me stony with love

Now this latest birth
a division
of what I had by what I am
by day I live in the corners carefully watching
my power frozen
at night I unfurl the memory of hair across the pillow
strong limbs covered by its shadow
I shape it carefully
I am tender towards it
as I had once been ruthless and sure
now I am something
else—
a being unfolding in the sparse strands
of night's slow gray

again a figure

a new thing

a creature unnamed and spinning

whatever heals left to the dreams I forget by sunrise

Intentions

I cup my hands and am told
to fill them with my intentions
for my practice.

Last class I filled them
with my mother's whole body
I felt her weight in them
by the end of the class
I had placed her back inside me
palm to palm.

I really don't know how to write a poem anymore
maybe it is the distress of the day
the air always being emptied
of meaning
or because we are shaped
by lies.

Now I look down at my cupped hands
and my mother is not there
I bend my neck, head to my chest
I acknowledge
the empty hands
I acknowledge her body
firmly in the hands of strangers
elsewhere—
this is the true vigil, this before-death.

When she hears my voice on the phone
I'm loved. She doesn't need to know anything
about me, about my day, about my children—
she says *oh* and *oh* and *oh*.

She is the woman who was once my mother.
She is the mother of my intention.

My hands still cupped, waiting to be filled
far from the hands that strain to hold her.

She is the woman
who was once my mother
untangling my hair with a wide comb, my hips held firmly
between her thighs as she tugged at the tight knots.

Communion

When we had church in the woods last autumn

wind whipping our faces

noses wet with the cold

we all squeezed our padded hips close on the benches
to keep the freezing air from between us

we shortened the readings

we only said the parts that were important

cold air rested on the hard round of bread and I was glad

Communion would be more than the cardboard
wafer melting with refrigerator taste
into the back of my throat

       the priest's breath rose in a cloud as she blessed it

and her fingers

       cramped from the cold

tore in

then she placed the crumbling portions in palms we cupped
to save it from the wind

and we each ate our bread nearly whole
feeding ourselves like she-birds
delivering the worm into the waiting nest of our own mouths

we smiled a little at each other

not to be caught obviously chewing the body of Christ.

Tattoo After Sophmore Year in College

Now a 19th-century pistol
a bar maid might have carried for protection
hugs her flank, holstered to
the long and shorter breaths she takes.
Flower buds cascade beneath her breast,
somewhat visible beneath an athletic bra.
The skin still looks taut and sore,
needled black lines almost purple.

She's eager to know what I think of it.
I remember the undyed skin, smooth and tan
where there's now a gun loaded with blooms;
and I can hear it, too, the woods echo
with other girls like you.
May the mountains straight reply
and keep you safe.

III

Classroom Poem

My back to the small lecture hall
and its now quiet swivel chairs
only the hum of the fluorescents dimming
I followed my hand with my eyes
as I wiped the shiny white surface clean of the red dry erase marker
making new shapes as my hand passed through letters I'd drawn,
and arrows, underlines doubled,
thinking as my hand moved what they might have thought
having read little of the novel, perhaps only knowing
the parts I'd sung out to them with so much joy—and now my joy
            was just mine
and for some reason all I could think was happy happy happy
to be in that room, loving having taught more than teaching,
knowing the air it had left in the room better even than other knowledge.
How to explain the silvery strain their boredom or wonder
had left in my lungs, in the stretch of my torso
as I reached to wipe the uppermost notes clear
as if also wiping clear the me who had longed once
to be in that place in which I now stood.

Voices of the Dead

I'm careful around the voices of the dead,
do not want their words to follow me loosely,
gamely like the eyes of some crowd of teenage boys
at the corner smoking and laughing,
the girl in me no longer apparent as I near them.

I've waited until dark some days, until the house hums
with the sounds of sleep, and the dog, too, out like a light,
to find a brief way back in, to listen for their words more precisely,
but it is as though sound curves in on me—the places they sought
    in my home,
attic and garden, just places now without them tapping the table,
    sighing,

digging or writing. Mornings I lean against the kitchen counter
coffee in hand, the steam flicking a little bitterness against my lip.
    Not a sign
but I take it that way. A trail of burnt coal from last night's dinner
    weirdly
marks several steps of the porch that the dog inspects, moves past.
August summer flames early today, then releases, then rises again.

At Home Depot 15 Years After Your Death

When you said listen for me
did you say angels? —but I insist
to remember it this way, to pin it,
thumbtack fighting the crumbling plaster.

You said you would BE
and we wouldn't have to miss you.

You must have known I would believe you.

So at the Home Depot gardening section today,
such a late spring, I cannot find the tomatoes,
and when I do I'm weirdly upset.
I know you would not like them, spindly and diseased.
I can hear you.

Is that the way of my work these days,
conjuring you into existence
when even the borders around houses and rocket ships
are beginning to slip from our grasp
and everyone is leaving the party before they're asked to?

Mortality, doors shutting behind me, the parent gone
who brought me here,
who willed me, was surprised by my awful first cry, named me,
startled at my fingers wet and rounding over their knuckle.

When She Told Me She Had Cancer

We were drinking coffee at Mystic Roasters
and I thought oh, she wasn't avoiding me because
we weren't entertaining enough at our last meal together.
She's dying. And she didn't know if we'd known each other well enough
to let me in, to die along with me in friendship.

And then I tried not to cry because she was so brave
and showed me her little packet of chemotherapy tied
like the old sanitary diapers our mothers had to wear
strapped by belts and pins. We laughed but inside I knew

and she knew that now that I had found her so late in life
I would have to learn to say goodbye to her. I could almost not bear
finishing my coffee, and saying goodbye to her for the day
and I went home to read the blog her husband had started. It was

a closed circuit and you had to be invited into it. A little
technical glitch so that I couldn't Google out the name of it, *What's up
With Ann?* So I Facebooked her the message, *I can't get in*, and then
she wrote me back the link, the link that let me in.

Shavasana

We came to the same pose each class,
lowering our rumps onto sticky mats,
stretching one leg and then another,
running our spines against the matted floor
until we were like that, down on our backs:
the pose of death, the pose of the corpse,
corpus. And you were held by one you were told
was dying. And that you were told
was the only difference between us
as we relaxed toes, ankles, let our thighs
roll and fall where they would, breathed
as we fell into our temporary dying.
We rarely lay beside each other—you were on time
and would have a good spot across the room;
I'd be nearest the door where I could hear
the drumbeat of the weight room
or the tv's blaring in Cardio. I did not think
shavasana, corpse pose, though it was said over and over,
I thought, after yoga, maybe I can have coffee with Ann.

Last Visit

I carved a perfect 20 minutes into a Monday day of errands,
grazed through the yard for any color that could be presented and
    look alive and stuffed the flowers and semi-weeds into a big glass
    mason jar.
And I wondered if after they were done
watching each homegrown summer weed breathe its last,
each hydrangea petal flap its little blue wink and wilt,
if they would mark the jar with washable eraser
with big letters, J-U-L-I-A, as they'd marked each plastic tub of food
    I'd sent to store for busy days.
I'd thought I could leave them on the porch with my note that by then
    my friend was probably too exhausted to even read,
but the door seemed slightly opened,
and I yearned to see her.
Standing at the door I knew why I had come: I'd never hear her laugh
    again at something she found ridiculous.
I knocked and a woman with a similar glow opened the door, her sister.
I stood a room away from where she lay, and uttered *sorry sorry sorry*,
I was not part of the inner circle, I was neighbor or acquaintance,
    and maybe
just a tiny bit more than that,
and Beccah asked her if she could do it,
and I heard her voice, so strained and pure, the stutter nearly gone,
Oh Julia, yes, Julia.
And when I saw her I knew that if her sister had not called her Ann
    I would not have known who she was.
Cancer had taken her beautiful somewhat masculine face, that of
    Hollywood's female leads of the 40s, mouth made for the width
    of red that made lips maddeningly gorgeous in black and white,
so I tried instead to listen to the voice inside her voice, the one that
    I'd remembered,

a little gravelly and warm. I was worried to hold her hand too long, or to kiss her, because then she'd know I knew. I didn't want my shock to be her mirror, but she must have known I knew that it was time.

And then we said goodbye.

Labor After Two Decades

They are killing her again.

Frieda Hughes, "The Mother"

In the early years, my legs, like the hind quarters of an animal,
would collapse beneath me. Most days you would have to say
I wasn't coping well. The cupboard doors open, I'd sway

into its hollow as though to put my whole body in there

—the toddler: doe eyes watching me, raspberry lips, tiny glittering teeth,
a small girl bracing—does she remember?

how I couldn't lift my fork some days? couldn't
move? couldn't do?

Is it too much for you some days I'd ask any other mother
and the *no* like a whip against my skin and how
I knew it was coming though I'd ask again and again.

Around 5 p.m. each night
my breath would go faster rounder and I could
no longer look at the clock, afraid then and there I'd burst,
loosening the love I'd learned as a child
into sharp slivers
barely visible on the faux brick linoleum floor.

That year I bought a copy of the diaries of Sylvia Plath
flipped to the middle of the book and realized I could not do it
had no right, had no
vision large enough to hold
the both of us. This was the first book
I've ever thrown away.

Winter Walk

The ridge of snow overlays the last major *yeah*
escaped from out under my breath,
now just the deep of cold.

On our walk the dog collapses in joy at the sniff of another dog.
Circle squeal.
        All night my hands
had twitched under covers, dried out
by the heart of heat we pump and burn,
a dump of oil on oil.
            Universe consuming universe—our clamped up souls
have no choice.

The bird in the morning streams through the air,
a delight of brown wing flashing against blue,
a tease flying from bare branch to bare branch,
dog half crazy with desire to hunt it down.

He, too, clamped, the leash a tangle between us.
Sidewalk indistinguishable from street,
walkways from porch stairs.
There is no way to go I tell him,
standing between dirty barricades of snow.

We slip in between the mess—my boots and his paws
churning together against small caves of salt, dirt,
black-brown snow, frozen tire marks and bands of ice.
In morning light at least it's all crystal.
And somehow we're led back
to the center of the drift.

Walk in the Neighborhood

It's already too late.
I'm laughing, talking to a friend on my cell

while I steer the dog around the corner,
forgetting I'll be passing this house of grief.

I see the man crafting his small lawn,
grass blades so perfectly straight and green

they seem cut with an exacto knife to fit the edges.
Yesterday he told me his son had died the week before.

And though I don't know his name
we embraced and cried.

Today I move my ear away from the cell
and we smile differently now, me apologetic to be living,

him apologetic to be curating his green patch
with the young man gone a week from this strange world.

El Cementerio, Villa El Salvador, Perú

Dear María Elena Moyano Delgado,
we have finished saying our prayers
over your tomb—"*Siempre en el Corazón de Villa El Salvador.*"
Sister Claire guides us through the rubble,
shows us your new neighbors living in makeshift houses,
canvas, tin, cardboard. No running water, no electricity.
Sand turns to dirt and mud beneath our feet. Are we
touring *El Cementerio* or trespassing on a private way?
We American visitors *tsk* our disapproval at the way the sacred is
    squandered here,
or we *tsk* at the squatters themselves, their children chasing wild dogs
    down the road,
or we *tsk* at what poverty and an absent government force
the living to do, build in the refuse of the unfinished cemetery,
taking their places where tombs and plots should be planted.
Some poverty is ugly and some seems brave.
I am not sure, María; it is hard to get it right here
where so many *compañeros* before you
hoisted walls and roofs just yards from the sacred ancient grounds
of Pachacámac, site of Peru's earliest and kindest gods.
Or those who came in this last century
to create your Villa of the Savior. The rubble and trash
grow around the site, but the dark stone of your face
smiles at us. To your left and right more victims of *Sendero Luminoso's*
    hatred,
like you, mothers, fathers. Behind you, the stacked tombs of children
form high walls of blue and pink, framing your sacred space.
Even after they tried to kill everything in you, dynamiting your body
    after your death,
El Cementerio births a new sector of Villa
growing without tenderness,
nudging your bones deeper into its core.

Envelope Poem

*Emily Dickinson sent this minuscule two-inch-long
pencil . . . in a letter to the Bowles, "If it had no pencil,
/ Would it try mine —" wryly nudging them to write. It
was enveloped in a letter folded into thirds horizontally,
pinned closed at each side.*

Jan Bervin, "Studies in Scale" in *Emily
Dickinson The Gorgeous Nothings*

Like the poet, my mother wrote letters all her life,
puzzling messages half in pencil half in ink;
she'd tape them laboriously instead of pin them,
each note almost the same.
Instead of a pencil hinting for us to write
a $5 bill sometimes crimped into a small square
and when most mischievous, a single dollar
folded many times and
have a cup of coffee
see you soon god willing
scratched
inside a greeting card
from a mission she'd given money to
or on a quarter of a blue-lined sheet of loose-leaf,
and wrapped and etched on that
another note,
kisses and hugs marked in x's and o's.
Each edge of card or sheet snugly taped,
the envelope itself double sealed,
especially the minuscule space between
where the envelope's glue ends
and no sealant lives.
Now the notes addressed to my kids,
and like Emily's command to the Bowles to write back:
take your mother out for coffee
buy something god bless.

A Song for 4th Grade

You were that still girl in the room
arms rare twigs reaching out
as though the rest of you'd been consumed
by fire or water. Your eyes focused, sharp.

Your arms rare twigs barely reaching out
you seemed to be calling me to you
by fire or water. Your eyes focused and sharp
as if our friendship had always been in view.

You seemed to call me to you
wrapped my feelings in your dark wool sweater
as if our friendship had always been in view
and recess no longer torture.

We wrapped our feelings in woolen sweaters
everything we did so awkward teachers feared us.
At recess, no longer torture
we spoke our secret language. No one owned us.

Everything we did so awkward teachers feared us
thought we'd crack on contact.
Speaking our secret language, no one owned us.
We gathered weeds and flowers from the concrete.

Some days we thought we'd crack on contact
as though the rest of us had been consumed.
We'd gather weeds and flowers from the concrete.
You were that still girl in the room.

That Afternoon

Sharp rays of light and heat
too late in the day.

We puffed up the hill
into
yellow brilliance while even lightest
wildflowers sat dead-still in the still air.

Before one lone house
a sign warning us of hunters—
could we two be mistaken for deer?
laughing *yes*
looking down
at our drab shorts and tees.

In the breadth of real time
I guess we shared
some fractions.
News of our children, your divorce pressed later
into emails
Boston to NY
I read and wrote on Amtrak.
Another email flurry
when you said you'd pulled my book off a shelf to read
dashed before Christmas.

Some element of friendships that drop from the sky
gift us and flee like that—
an image of us in a landscape strange to both of us
now absent of us there,
and of us here, too.

On Helen's Return

Her problem is that she's too beautiful.

A friend

I don't like rain and everyone says
oh, I love the rain. No. Or the fog
just someone keeping visibility from me
playing with me. No I don't like it. Or snow if it starts
to accumulate at the arcs of the windshield wipers.
No to ice, to the slick and dangerous
underneath me. I've experimented with the Yes
but end up saying yes to the wrong things
the wrong men who want to kill me. I say yes
to the sun, the hazard of light that blinds me
yes to the web my body makes that leaves
no trace of me in the ground.
If I passed this way again or didn't
no one would know, just a shadow.
After disaster, the telephone lines are up again
though nobody uses them. The voice in my throat
is loose again, too, oh to use it well. The paper makes incisions
in my palms that sting. Even my skin can sing
its little pains but the throat so numb with
the fog of what we say or lose. I make
the food I shouldn't tonight. They say
I eat the hard-boiled bones of my ancestors.
Well I wish I did. What god would stop me anyhow?

My Ithaca

Κι αν πτωχική την βρεις, η Ιθάκη δεν σε γέλασε.
Έτσι σοφός που έγινες, με τόση πείρα,
ήδη θα το κατάλαβες η Ιθάκες τι σημαίνουν.

C. P. Cavafy, "Ithaca"

And if you find her poor, Ithaca did not deceive you.
As wise as you'll have become, with so much experience,
you'll have understood, by then, what these Ithacas mean.

tr. Daniel Mendelsohn

I close my eyes to see the dark-tarred road,
the steep decline all sand blown and stony.
My thin legs spin faster beneath me as I run,
more than my body can control.
Falling hard—contact!
knees sliding scraping bleeding,
then your hands firm around my calves,
and the cold peroxide gleaming and bubbling.

Later, or days later
we settle onto our spots on the beach,
your body gripped in its Latex suit,
the flowered bathing cap
encircling your face.
Goddess—I liked watching
the flapping petals of that helmet.

We had entered the water together—
you, magically: your feet
bound by the rubber swimming slippers
felt no pain.

Back then I am your daughter, certain of my place
watching the sun envelop you.

You've prayed the prayer of Ithaca
all your life—
the return, the journey a good one.

You, too, remember holding
my hand—?

I think you can
but I am not sure.

Now, in bed, when your eyes close
my hands warm your cool skin.

If you are my Ithaca
who is yours? The sister?
the favorite brother? the brilliant
blue-eyed husband?

I want to say you see me there, too,
will see me, catch me, the thin
brown girl.

The speed of light that joins all time—

You squeeze back, say *oh*.
What of the body
reveals itself in that small sound? What one-eyed monster,
what terrible storm that could ever
frighten you?

End of Semester Visit from My Student and We Speak of Death

I'm afraid for the summer
she says. *Too many memories.*
Back home some will remember
more of him, some nothing. She is
trying not to cry.

Her 4-beat rhyming couplets flow now
with this new death
into *chemo like water in his veins.*

I tell her about calling
my phantom father
when I'm driving home from work,
forgetting he is dead,

and then I sit very still
far from my stack of unfiled papers
at the round table in the middle of my office.
I sip a Dunk's latte
while she recites a poem for her 5 extra points.

The poem isn't by anyone famous;
it's by a classmate about a girl
waiting at a window
for someone who never arrives.

I know the poem is about her grief.
My back is to the oversized window she's facing,
its panes grim with dirt,
and though it must be pried
it can still be opened.

A shadow floats between us,
a paper-doll cut from my body or hers.

She stands, ready to go.
What tune her dead boyfriend
will make in her ear next I don't know.
Grief sucks I say,
and she seems grateful though

it could have gone either way.
I rise with her but I'm unable to
move toward her. We stand still
in our own places and listen
to the loud end-of-semester
whoops in the hallway,
the relief of a bad exam
a paper finally submitted

and the room feels smaller when she leaves
and unable to hold me.

To New York

How a city can give you up
give you away
how you could once own a city
how you fear it—can't feel it
inside you anymore—
the streets are strange as though
their concrete you once
bounced your soles on
block after geometrical block
now are empty halls that echo
with your stranger's gait.
In any season, in this season of heat
the air is thicker than you remember
the skyline jags with new shapes.
It was never kind. It was
never mine. All the museums seem
larger, seem to frame what's outside.
I can only remember inside.
The slap of the East River
its manicured piers one fancy hat
on top of another. The exposed brick
dimly lit, $40-an-entrée boutique restaurants
shredding their light into a street
once dark and empty below the Bowery.
Citicorp's façade at twilight
a gray-green spider of light
right before we'd meet for drinks in the funny
mall space we'd never seen in a city.
The heavy roar of the E train that appeared
without a schedule
and the F train's glowy orange seats.

And 14th Street's dollar stores and the grimness
of Union Square Park you would not walk through but around.
New York, I got lost on my way to the Strand last winter.
I was not wearing black.
I was not guided by anything I know.

IV

Day Begins

5:40 a.m. and the light is yesterday's light
or rather today opens a replica
of the day before
or the day has slipped not yet begun
into the pocket of yesterday
seamless and quiet in its tucking in
the dog pushes the bedroom door ajar
and like the day, slips in
stretches rear up, head down
head up, rear down
patters and clicks to where my hand extends
and receives the pat to his side
the lick of my palm across his back
and exits. I watch to see if something new
has arrived. I realize
it is time to breathe, to patch the day before yesterday
into yesterday and that day into today
to make a plane, a simple level surface
a way toward day-stream
a not beginning to begin, a clasping and a pinning down.

Cleaning the Groceries in the Time of Covid-19

Porous or non-porous, the skin of a melon?
the skin of my hands rinsed and soaped and rinsed
porous darkening olive winking through suds with a scaly grudge
non-porous the kitchen faucet, the sink,
the fridge, porous the plastic bag?
and the melon, porous and clean with the soap of my hands?
the counter non-porous sprayed with the infectious ammonia liquid
the liquid like the cough, porous as air—thins and cuts through.

Porous the windy apron flouncing
against my mother's quick legs. Red-ribboned cotton porous
and non-porous the spatula of stainless steel
poking the veal cutlets, porous soaking in the oil
porous the scent of basil and darkened breadcrumbs
the olive pool porous, also non-porous liquid and thick.

Non-porous the bungalow at the bottom of the hill
front door and back door screens bowed and butterflied
air in the flaps of the morning. Porous, the 1960s wallpaper—
figures of winking cowboys in the cream-colored silt
non-porous the crumbling plaster it clings to
non-porous the club glass filled to the top.

Porous or non-porous the plastic bag holding the apples?
non-porous the bowl I slip them in. Porous the wind
non-porous, our lungs breathing a shape
porous and hidden, the skin of my hand the sponge of the illness
the shed of the skin, the water filling the sink.

Watching Church on Facebook Live, Not Live, in the Time of the Pandemic

I get up too late to see the sunrise.
My Easter vigil begins at 9 a.m.
I sing off-key.
I make the coffee.
I light the candle I found in the bathroom called "sand and fog."
I am moving, not concentrating;
I have many windows open on the screen.

Easter is always cold here.
The lector is un-mic'd so the words feel broken.
She is reading the strange passage,
in the middle of the valley, dry bones. I read along out loud
as my non-believing husband moves in and out of the kitchen
the bones rattling loving me
                              but not this.

Poem for My Daughter in the Pandemic

Within weeks her city will be burning its two fevers
as will the city of my adoption.
Her city was my city. She is vacuuming
in her sports bra and leggings,
lifting the vacuum across the wide couch. Happy, temporarily,
her roommates have fled for a suburban house in Florida;
the apartment will stay clean.
She is not even breathless wielding the wide vacuum.
The phone moves with her. I'm dizzy with the frame's movement.
I'm propped on a shelf. I watch a light fixture on her ceiling
as I listen to a vacuum noise, a voice.

While we talk, I stare at a photo printed on plain paper
thumbtacked to the bulletin board behind my computer,
curled at its edges. She is 12 in it, just days before her first period
and future dull aches, fevers, and tears without definite source.
Her back is to me, long hippy skirt and dark braids both in mid-swing
meadow grass at her ankles, little brother following behind her.

Task complete she slides me over to her galley kitchen,
propped I imagine on the ledge of her backsplash,
pulls a box from the freezer, unwraps it—
crinkle sound rushes through the phone line,
slam of microwave and fridge—
disappears from my frame, returns
fork in hand, looks around, breaks a plastic seal and the steam
rises from the white bowl.

Now the tour: window frame taped up from an attempted
break in, cracked fixture in the bathroom,
its long leak. She is calm. In a later phone call I'll learn
when Manhattan goes dark, she locks herself up in her bedroom,
the eeriness of midtown's empty streets a shudder

until light breaks. At her age I was married,
the subway fare a token, pressed and brassy and worn in.

The girl in the center of danger holds me in her palm now,
waves to me, the red button I hit that ends our night together
nearly caress. I watch her climb through the meadow's grass.
I can only see the back of her head,
the beautiful hair swinging.

The Poets Are Writing About Birds

Everyone is writing about birds
        flying, or their bones
brittle, smooth, frail, buried, splintered, their bones.
Or their feathers lost
among wet leaves. Floating.
It's as if in quarantine
they think they [finally] have something in common
with the starling caught in someone's attic or rather
they remember desire as a way
to distinguish themselves.

These are the poets who would have felt
it was trite to claim to be birds
to be like birds
landed on high wires

but now they bring out their bitters,
their chemistry sets, to make
the poem with the birds in it—

but housed here the soothing air

isn't hard for me. I don't need birds to realize
I don't long for flight.
I know the birds I watch now,
so many, are not missing us,
it's finally their sky—their light.

The streets are theirs now, too—they
hop—isn't it comical to see them
on the wet sidewalk
on the lowest bough of the young tree
so close to the dog's dumb breath?

#2020

Most days this year
I have eluded the sun
or granted it shape
in small bits inside my study
through shades I
climbed on my desk
to unfurl with a thump into the sill
or to pull up and adjust with an old binder clip

For one month of 2020 we rented
a small perfect house and I woke and slept
with the sun's passage
from harbor sleight of hand
early morning to
its bedding down at night
with other stars

Today I watch the sun's light
hit my neighbors' rooftops
that crowd my backyard patch—
I like the shapes and colors
of their asphalt hues—
slate gray, dull gray, silver,
terracotta red, and the vinyl siding
that bounces the light without absorbing it

March light grows distinct. It's
Sunday 6 a.m. and I wake to
the strangeness of what money
can and cannot buy, what time means
in different hands, who culls
the stretch of a horizon
and who must save up to see it

The Flower Moon

is best seen in the early morning
but I stare down instead of up
light shimmers through the slick pool of rain

& in it, odd blooms: Boston's antibodies
nestled in blue paper masks flattened and wet
broken loops of Mardi Gras beads stranded
lost business cards & thin-skinned surgical gloves beside them

as though the whole of an emergency room had shed its skin
everything needed for the pandemic
spilling off curbs, crushed into the silvery granite

Prayer

I have written to you before
and though I have tried to wait

I am impatient in my prayers
and I do not know where my praise ends up.

I know I must include it with the ask, send it forth
to the great goddess. Maybe if I lighted

candles as I did through Europe as
a college student, saying my mother's name,

my aunt's name in various country churches and city cathedrals.
I never prayed for my father or my boyfriend.

It was not as though they were not worth
the coin I pressed into the copper boxes

and listened for—the clang I heard, coin to bottom of the box, or
    duller coin to coin.
But that they did not hear the call those prayers made as well

as the women who had tended me would. When I said my mother's
    name
her life would rise to me and to you, sweet goddess, in our steadfast
    breath,

and she would know I was fine, without the help of cellphone or email.
I must believe in the prayers again, offered

with make-believe coins in make-believe boxes.
Maybe this poem is the box into which I press the coin,

these beads of words themselves the prayer, *mumble mumble,*
the sounds are love and must transpire, but the prayer is so much

bigger, a terrible request of Mary and Elizabeth
who also must be Jesus, Father, and Holy Ghost.

It is a prayer of only-pleading, and not only for the dear women who
     loved me,
but it must attend to the mess of the world,

hear the terrible unformed cries, little yelps in the universe,
and speed something like, not recovery because

who would want to return to what churned this?
But to something like health of bones, of muscle, of lungs,

of love for the other
whom I am yet to meet.

The New York Times Publishes 1000 Names

> *I don't know about you, but I'm ready for something*
> *to be different. This staying at home, not knowing*
> *what's going to happen next, worrying, not sleeping*
> *well . . . it's tiring.*
>
> Email from my yoga teacher, May 26, 2020

Let us be tired.

Let us stay and arrange the coffee mugs on a new shelf;
let us stare at the dog;

let us roam around the house forgetting
what we needed to do next. Let us

read the 1000 names knowing they are only
a portion of what ails us—. All morning let's read them.

Let us read the names out loud.
Let us be interested in how the *Times* defines a life and

how we do. How we do. This is the virus and that is the gun.
This is the virus and that is the knee on the neck. This is the
vigil and that is the vigil. This is the breath not taken
and that is the breath not taken. This is the storm and that is the cough.
This is the mask and that is the placard.

Let us hear the fear in a neighbor's cough;
let us hear the fear in a siren.

Let us vigil, let us watch here on our knees, in the sunlight.

Let us remember to kneel in the sunlight, 8 minutes, 20 minutes, a
lifetime.

Let us reject athletic trainers and yoga teachers and meditation leaders
and priests and poets. They mean well. They mean

to get us back into "it"—they are here for "us."

Let us stop feeling relieved if we do not have

underlying conditions. We have underlying conditions.

I Buried the Virus in a Time Machine

Last night I read a sutra to calm me down—
the body loves its cells, the body is an accident
of muscle and flesh, the body is really made of
gold and silver and the sun, moon, and stars.

But does the body love its traveled self, the cells
that multiply, divide and visit other parts of the body's self?
(I want to bury the virus, the fear of the virus
in a sweet little wooden time machine—pluck its grip
even from the ones who've died.) I know this kind of love

is perversion of what the sutra meant but how can we not
see the lamb of sacrifice and complacence in the eyes
of the time machine—homemade with an insignificant
brass lock? Stave the virus at least if not bury it? I see flocks

and flocks of time machines—these are wooden boxes, little
accidents that will be wormed into, interfered with. I've made
some miscalculation, busy with my loving body, I have missed
the real danger. Now all my time machines carrying the virus

of the dead and then of some of the living sit in the quiet meadow.
They are staring at me and I am lost in the thought of
this impossible containment—what protects us from each other
is NOT this ability to hold back, to discover in

another time and place the body's enemies. I know this
and steel myself to the fact—those green gremlin GIFs always
seem to be smiling at us from all ports and hills—I climbed
Assisi's hill when I was young and can't remember anything

unless I see a photograph of someone else's journey. And yet
St. Francis is a face I recall there—a time machine, too. Who

will protect them? The ones who walk through the trails of
unburied boxes and open them? this is not an ontological

question. Some will arrive on skateboards. Some will build
highways to get there. Some pinched memory will light
someone else's way. They'll say, this is the hill on which
another human had a vision. But these are just words

substituting for light, and in the end disregarding light
altogether, just creating darkness through the white space
taking a stand while the cells of my body do what they want,
multiply and worry.

In New England's February I Worry About What the Crocuses Will Tell Us

Any minute now,

betrayed by a single day or two of false spring,

crocus-bulbs will vibrate

just beneath the frozen earth

and startle the frigid air.

They'll poke through a later-blooming beauty bush,

or circle an overgrown ivy's root that's upended the slate walk,

their light purples and yellows insinuating

even as the cold air will likely descend on them again.

They want to be our sign of spring, of all that's passed,

buried in the cold ground,

so who am I to forecast their rising up

and their eventual and premature death?

We've made it to this point, but I can see now

that I am on the lookout for a one-year sign

to mark the day when days became more days

and the pandemic had killed what then felt like many.

The crocus will have a lot to carry this year,

I don't know if it will be able to—with its very short life—

bear up under all that hope and terror.

Demented Days: One Year into the Pandemic

Waking itself is a kind of small chore—
one that brings me satisfaction from having done it.
Eyes open, I let the daily morning flash of heat
rise from my shoulders to the top of my head, resolve until
I'm chilled again. I stretch, find the nightgown
like a wide-open artichoke preening around my ribs,
cotton socks still crumpled at the bottom of the mattress,
I unfurl the fronds of nightgown,
I'm a slender bird again, dig with my toes
to pull the socks toward my hands,
retrieve sweats from the floor, my bandana under my pillow.
Movement is slow but not methodical, more like
dream movement. I am dressed in something but what is it?
I'm in a house with floors but where are they?
I swing my legs over the side of the bed. My feet touch the floor,
I venture standing, and then walking, two legs beneath me
a marvel,
and I begin to imagine the filling of the house
with my next things and the things after that.

I'm Receiving Now

I'm receiving now, arms bare and wide,
the rain on the window, the plot without an ending

I can understand. Even now, the temperature outside to inside,
the walls a blank cream color, not a shimmer or a way to go.

I'm receiving now, all the excuses and pardons,
all the shirred edges, the unmade beds, the photographs

unidentified and yellowing, maybe my mother's friend, my father's
cousin. In the middle of a dark road the oil slicks, the cars passing

but not arriving. Who is going anywhere? I'm receiving now
the gifts left on the doorstep, no it's the mail, boxed and damp

in the cold rain. I'm receiving now my paces,
my permission. The flood at my feet is wild with its own

abundance. How silly I've been. The furniture cramped and full
of dust and blankets, the couch worn and creasing its leather face,

my hands extended. I'm receiving all the grief here it is here it is.

NOTES ON THE POEMS

"Maternal Half-Life" is written in response to the mass shooting on June 12, 2016 when Omar Mateen killed 49 people and injured 53 at the Pulse Nightclub in Orlando, Florida, a gay bar. There was some speculation that Mateen may have occasionally frequented the bar, suggesting he himself may have been gay. The epigraph for the poem is from a caption defining half-life found at *A Linda Hall Library Exhibition*, "The Atomic Age" at https://atomic.lindahall.org/what-is-meant-by-half-life.html

The title, "A Member of the Poor," is inspired by the title of Gwendolyn Brooks' poem, "The Lovers of the Poor."

"a brief history" refers to several historical markers for Italian Americans, including the lynching March 14, 1891 of 11 Italian immigrants in New Orleans, and its link to President Harrison's proclamation of Columbus Day in 1892, intended to be a one-time holiday to placate Italian Americans.

The penultimate line of "Tattoo After Sophomore Year in College" borrows a line from Emily Dickinson's poem "My life had stood – a loaded gun" (J754, Fr764).

"When She Told Me She Had Cancer", "Shavasana" and "Last Visit" are in memory of Ann Gallager (Nov. 11, 1962–August 14, 2013).

"El Cementerio" commemorates the life of María Elena Moyano Delgado (November 29, 1958–February 15, 1992). She was a Peruvian community organizer and activist of Afro-Peruvian descent. She was assassinated by the Shining Path (*Sendero Luminoso*), a brutal insurgent movement that reigned and terrorized Peruvian peasants, trade union workers and many others. Her tomb fronts the cemetery in Villa, but much of the cemetery grounds have been usurped by squatters looking for housing. During the 1980s and early '90s, María Elena helped organize the settlers of Villa El Salvador, a grassroots urban development outside of the capital of Lima, Peru. To this day, Villa is pointed out as an example of what is possible for poor people to achieve in terms of self-organization. And yet, many of the "sectors" or neighborhoods of Villa are still severely underserved and the spirit of settling by squatting continues, even in the cemetery that honors Villa's political heroes.

"Cleaning the Groceries in the Time of Covid-19" was written early in the pandemic when we did not know how Covid-19 was transmitted. We spent much time watching YouTube videos about how best to clean our groceries before putting them away.

The "two fevers" in "Poem for My Daughter in the Pandemic" refers to the Covid-19 pandemic and the protests against police brutality following the killing of George Floyd, Jr.

"*The New York Times* Publishes 1000 Names" refers to the May 24, 2020 issue of *The New York Times* in which the paper published the names of 1000 of the 10,000 Americans we had so far lost to Covid-19, with their brief bios. The names filled the front page to impress upon us how many pages we would need to name all 10,000 American lives we had lost by that point. A day after, on May 25, 2020, George Floyd was brutally murdered by a policeman during his arrest. His murder felt like the last straw of a violent year of brutal killings—Ahmaud Arbery, Breonna Taylor, and so many others, reminding us that the pandemic wasn't our only emergency or our only failing as a culture. On May 26, 2020, I received the email from my yoga instructor that I quote from in the epigraph to the poem. No doubt it was meant to be a benign and helpful message about Covid-19 and quarantining.

ACKNOWLEDGMENTS

I am grateful to the editors of the following journals and anthologies in which versions of some of the poems in this volume have appeared:

Apple Valley Review: "Envelope Poem"

The Big Windows Review: "Bird Walk"

B O D Y: "A Lesson from My Father About Manure"

Cider Press Review: "Poem for My Daughter in the Pandemic"

Exit 7: "Communion"

Global Quarantine Museum, Pendemics Journal: "The Poets Are Writing About Birds" and "Cleaning the Groceries in the Time of Covid-19"

Gravel: "A Song for Fourth Grade", "Thoughts About Hunger on a Morning Walk"

Hags on Fire: "Hot Flash"

Itallan Americana: "Marriage Bed", "Walk in the Neighborhood"

I-70 Review: "Intentions" appeared as "More on Yoga Practice"

Juked: "Classroom Poem"

Lily Poetry Review: "I'm Receiving Now"

MER Online: "Shavasana" and "Charlotte's Zinnias"

Mom Egg Review: "Labor After Two Decades"

Newtown Literary: "End of Semester Visit from My Student and We Speak of Death", "Before This", "Tattoo in Sophomore Year"

Nimrod International Journal of Prose and Poetry : "Mercy", "Octave", "Some Loved Object"

The Ocean State Review: "Maternal Half-Life", "On Helen's Return"

On the Seawall: "Prayer" and "Community Garden"

Ovunque Siamo: "Long Distance" and "Winter Walk"

Pangyrus: "*The New York Times* Publishes 1000 Names"

Paterson Literary Review: "My Ithaca"

Plath Poetry Project: "Voices of the Dead" which appears as "After Plath's Burning the Letters" and "*Love* Visits Us"

Ploughshares: "Beginnings, December" appeared as "Beginnings, December 20, 2018"

San Pedro River Review: "To New York"

Smokey Blue Literary and Arts Magazine: "a brief history" and "At Home Depot 15 Years After Your Death"

Talking Writing: "Faculty Development Workshop"

"El Cementerio, Villa El Salvador, Peru" appeared in *Sharing the Earth: An International Environmental Justice Reader.* Eds. Elizabeth Ammons and Modhumita Roy. University of Georgia Press, 2016.

"Faculty Development Workshop" and "Maternal Half-Life" were reprinted in *Welcome to the Resistance: Poetry as Protest.* Eds. Ona Gritz and Taylor Savath. South Jersey Culture & History Center, Stockton University Press, 2021.

"Walk in the Neighborhood" and "In New England's February I Worry About What the Crocuses Will Tell Us" were featured in the art & poetry exhibit, "Lines Connecting Lines 2022" at Urban Media Arts, Malden, MA, April–June, 2022. The cover art is taken from one of these works.

AND THANK YOU

To the Vermont Studio Center for the freedom of time to begin this work— and thank you to all the brilliant poets, writers, and visual artists I met there.

Many of the poems here had their first audience at the open mics of the Italian American Writers Association at I Am Books and on Zoom. Thank you for listening to all the early versions! To the many groups of poets, literary organizations and initiatives that sprung into action with workshops, readings, and write-ins that sustained so many of us as writers and citizens during the last few anxious years, among them: Megan and Lini at The Plath Poetry Project, Two Sylvias Press Online Poetry Retreat, Eileen Cleary's Revision Boot Camp, Maria Mazziotti Gillan's day-long poetry retreats, Licia Canton's Saturday morning write-ins.

To Regis College for a sabbatical, and to my students; I've been fed by your company, your curiosity, and your determination.

My deepest gratitude goes to the readers of this manuscript who provided invaluable feedback on individual poems or on the manuscript as a whole: Ann Keniston, Theodora Stratis, Ellen Goldstein, Rosemary Starace, Maria Lisella, and Jennifer Martelli. I'm grateful to Cammy Thomas, Adele Travisano, and Mary Ann McQuillan for their advice and continued support, and to Shana Hill, for helping so many of these poems find homes in beautiful publications.

One could not have a better editor than Nic Grosso at Bordighera Press who has shepherded this book with care, patience, and kindness. And to M.P. Carver, copyeditor extraordinaire, thank you for your discerning eye!

Love and thanks to my whole family, especially Ed, Renata, and Carl Kleifgen, my core and my source. And to our dear family companion, Vinny (2013–2022), who kept me company, and took many a walk with me. If I believed in muses, he'd be mine.

Grazie a tutti, un abbraccio.

ABOUT THE AUTHOR

In addition to *Our Lively Kingdom*, JULIA LISELLA is the author of two full-length collections of poetry: *Always* (WordTech Editions, 2014) and *Terrain* (WordTech Editions, 2007) and the chapbook, *Love Song Hiroshima* (Finishing Line Press, 2004). Her poems are widely anthologized, including most recently *Welcome to the Resistance: Poetry of Protest* (South Jersey Culture & History Center, Stockton University Press), *To Learn the Future: Poems for Teachers* (Scottish Poetry Library), and *Sharing the Earth: An International Environmental Justice Reader* (University of Georgia Press). Her work appears in *Ploughshares, Paterson Literary Review, Italian Americana, Ovunque Siamo, Pangyrus, Mom Egg Review, Nimrod, Alaska Quarterly Review, Antiphon, Ocean State Review, Literary Mama, Salamander, Prairie Schooner, Valparaiso,* and many others and she has had her work featured in such collaborative media exhibits as "Lines Connecting Lines 2022" and "TELEPHONE," an international art game. She has received residencies from the Vermont Studio Center, MacDowell, Millay, and Dorset colonies, and has received a number of grants from the Massachusetts Cultural Council to lead community poetry workshops. She holds an MA in Creative Writing from New York University and a PhD in English from Tufts. Her scholarship focuses on American women modernists. She is the co-editor of *Modernist Women Writers and American Social Engagement* (Lexington Books). She is Professor of English at Regis College in Massachusetts. She co-curates the Italian American Writers in Boston Literary Series at I Am Books in Boston's North End.

VIA Folios

A refereed book series dedicated to the culture of Italians and Italian Americans.

TAMBURRI. et al., Eds. *Italian Cultural Studies 2001*. Vol 33. Essays.
ELIZABETH G. MESSINA, Ed. *In Our Own Voices*.
  Vol 32. Italian/American Studies.
STANISLAO G. PUGLIESE. *Desperate Inscriptions*. Vol 31. History.
HOSTERT & TAMBURRI, Eds. *Screening Ethnicity*.
  Vol 30. Italian/American Culture.
G. PARATI & B. LAWTON, Eds. *Italian Cultural Studies*. Vol 29. Essays.
HELEN BAROLINI. *More Italian Hours*. Vol 28. Fiction.
FRANCO NASI, Ed. *Intorno alla Via Emilia*. Vol 27. Culture.
ARTHUR L. CLEMENTS. *The Book of Madness & Love*. Vol 26. Poetry.
JOHN CASEY, et al. *Imagining Humanity*. Vol 25. Interdisciplinary Studies.
ROBERT LIMA. *Sardinia/Sardegna*. Vol 24. Poetry.
DANIELA GIOSEFFI. *Going On*. Vol 23. Poetry.
ROSS TALARICO. *The Journey Home*. Vol 22. Poetry.
EMANUEL DI PASQUALE. *The Silver Lake Love Poems*. Vol 21. Poetry.
JOSEPH TUSIANI. *Ethnicity*. Vol 20. Poetry.
JENNIFER LAGIER. *Second Class Citizen*. Vol 19. Poetry.
FELIX STEFANILE. *The Country of Absence*. Vol 18. Poetry.
PHILIP CANNISTRARO. *Blackshirts*. Vol 17. History.
LUIGI RUSTICHELLI, Ed. *Seminario sul racconto*. Vol 16. Narrative.
LEWIS TURCO. *Shaking the Family Tree*. Vol 15. Memoirs.
LUIGI RUSTICHELLI, Ed. *Seminario sulla drammaturgia*.
  Vol 14. Theater/Essays.
FRED GARDAPHÈ. *Moustache Pete is Dead! Long Live Moustache Pete!*.
  Vol 13. Oral Literature.
JONE GAILLARD CORSI. *Il libretto d'autore. 1860 - 1930*. Vol 12. Criticism.
HELEN BAROLINI. *Chiaroscuro: Essays of Identity*. Vol 11. Essays.
PICARAZZI & FEINSTEIN, Eds. *An African Harlequin in Milan*.
  Vol 10. Theater/Essays.
JOSEPH RICAPITO. *Florentine Streets & Other Poems*. Vol 9. Poetry.
FRED MISURELLA. *Short Time*. Vol 8. Novella.
NED CONDINI. *Quartettsatz*. Vol 7. Poetry.
ANTHONY JULIAN TAMBURRI, Ed. *Fuori: Essays by Italian/American
  Lesbiansand Gays*. Vol 6. Essays.
ANTONIO GRAMSCI. P. Verdicchio. Trans. & Intro. *The Southern Question*.
  Vol 5. Social Criticism.
DANIELA GIOSEFFI. *Word Wounds & Water Flowers*. Vol 4. Poetry. $8
WILEY FEINSTEIN. *Humility's Deceit: Calvino Reading Ariosto Reading Calvino*.
  Vol 3. Criticism.
PAOLO A. GIORDANO, Ed. *Joseph Tusiani: Poet. Translator. Humanist*.
  Vol 2. Criticism.
ROBERT VISCUSI. *Oration Upon the Most Recent Death of Christopher Columbus*.
  Vol 1. Poetry.

CPSIA information can be obtained
at www.ICGtesting.com
Printed in the USA
JSHW022104120123
36121JS00002B/158